Microsoft Word is a word processing application designed by Microsoft. Microsoft Word, i.e. MS Word, is a part of the popular MS Office Package. Here you will find a good collection of Multiple Choice Questions to test your knowledge on Microsoft Word with answer. Most of the questions are applicable to all versions of MS Word (including Word 97-2003, 2007, 2010, XP, etc.). Sometimes these types of questions are asked as part of the general knowledge section of basic computer awareness and computer operation section.

MS Word Multiple Choice Questions - 100 Questions

And

MS Word Multiple Choice Questions - 100 Questions With Answer

MS Word Multiple Choice Questions - 100 Questions

1.Which bar shows the current position as far the text goes?

(A) Title bar

(B) Menu bar

(C) Scroll bar

(D) Status bar

2. Select all the text in MS Word document by

(A) Ctrl +S

(B) Ctrl+ 1

(C) Ctrl+ A

(D) Ctrl+ V

3. _____ is not a part of a MS Word document

(A) Quick access toolbar

(B) Start Menu button

(C) Home panel

(D) View option

4.The name of a word document displays in _____

(A) Ribbon

(B) Title bar

(C) Status bar

(D) Home tab

5.Each line represents how many letters in WordStar?

(A) 20

(B) 35

(C) 65

(D) 75

6.What is the blank space outside the printing area on a page?

(A) Clipart

(B) Margins

(C) Header

(D) Footer

7.Which of the following is an example of page orientation?

(A) Landscape

(B) Subscript

(C) Superscript

(D) A4

8.Formatting is performed on

(A) Text

(B) Table

(C) Menu

(D) Both (a) and (b)

9.Which of the following software is used for making resume?

(A) MS Excel

(B) MS Word

(C) Dev C

(D) Java

10.Press _____ to open the help window in MS word document.

(A) F1

(B) F2

(C) F9

(D) F11

11.Microsoft word is ____ software.

(A) Application

(B) Compiler

(C) System

(D) Programming

12.Which is not in MS word?

(A) Italic

(B) Magic tool

(C) Font

(D) Bold

13.____ cannot be used to work in MS Office.

(A) Joystick

(B) Scanner

(C) Light Pen

(D) Mouse

14.Which is not an edition of MS Word?

(A) MS Word 2003

(B) MS Word 2007

(C) MS Word 2010

(D) MS Word 1020

15.The ___ works with the standard Copy and Paste commands.

(A) View tab

(B) Paragraph dialog box

(C) Office Clipboard

(D) All of these

16.Line spacing is in the ____ of MS Word.

(A) Format tab

(B) View tab

(C) Insert tab

(D) Home tab

17.____ button reduces the window to an icon but word still remains active.

(A) Close

(B) Restore

(C) Maximize

(D) Minimize

18.Which term is not related with font?

(A) Font grammar

(B) Font color

(C) Font size

(D) Font face

19.____ Button brings word window to the maximum original size.

(A) Scroll

(B) Close

(C) Restore

(D) Minimize

20.What is the smallest width of a column?

(A) 0"

(B) 1"

(C) 0.5"

(D) 1.5"

21. Arial, Cambria, Verdana, Times New Roman are the name of ____

(A) Highlights

(B) Font face

(C) Text

(D) Alignment

22. What feature adjusts the top and bottom margins so that the text is centred vertically on the printed page?

(A) Vertical centering

(B) Vertical justifying

(C) Vertical adjusting

(D) Dual centering

23. The feature that keeps track of the right margin is

(A) Left justified

(B) Ragged right

(C) Right justified

(D) Find and replace

24. To make the selected text bold, the shortcut key is ____

(A) Alt+ B

(B) Shift+ B

(C) Ctrl+ B

(D) Space +H

25. Which file format cannot be added to a Word document?

(A) .png

(B) .jpg

(C) .kpz

(D) .gif

26. The process of removing unwanted part of an image is called

A. Hiding

B. Bordering

C. Cropping

D. Cutting

27. A detailed written description of the programming cycle and the program, along with the test results and a printout of the program is called ______

(A) Spreadsheets

(B) Reporting

(C) Output

(D) Documentation

28. A word processor would be used best to

(A) paint a picture

(B) workout income and expenses

(C) draw a diagram

(D) type a story

29. ______ are advanced features that can speed up editing or formatting you may perform often in a word document.

(A) Comment

(B) Track changes

(C) Ribbon

(D) Macros

30.To move data from one part of the document to another, following is used.

(A) Cut and Delete

(B) Cut and Paste

(C) Copy and Paste

(D) Copy and Undo

31.Go to end of a document, press ______

(A) Num Lock

(B) Tab

(C) End

(D) Home

32.Which of the following options is used to display information such a title, page number of the document?

(A) Auto Correct

(B) Header and Footer

(C) Thesaurus

(D) Insert Table

33.What is a set of unified design elements that provides a look for your document by using color, fonts and graphics?

(A) Highlight

(B) Format painter

(C) Line spacing

(D) Theme

34.To align right the selected text, the shortcut key is

(A) Ctrl + L

(B) Ctrl + R

(C) Ctrl + J

(D) Ctrl + U

35.To align left the selected text, the shortcut key is

(A) Ctrl + L

(B) Ctrl + R

(C) Ctrl + J

(D) Ctrl + U

36.To specify margins in word, the user has to select Page Setup option from which menu?

(A) Auto correct

(B) Edit

(C) File

(D) Table

37.What is a note or annotation that an author or review adds to a document?

(A) Comment

(B) Caption

(C) Header

(D) Footer

38.Microsoft Office Word creates a _____ for you when you press ENTER or the SPACEBAR after you type the address of an existing Web page.

(A) Hyperlink

(B) Header

(C) Chart

(D) Footer

39.Zoom in and out button is available on

(A) Scroll bar

(B) Home tab

(C) Page lauout tab

(D) View option toolbar

40.What is the blinking symbol on the screen that shows where the next character will appear?

(A) Cursor

(B) Delete key

(C) Arrow key

(D) Return key

41.The document can be zoom maximum upto

(A) 150%

(B) 200%

(C) 400%

(D) 500%

42.The bar at the top of the window that bears the name of the window is known as

(A) Title bar

(B) Menu bar

(C) Status bar

(D) Control panel

43.SmartArt is the feature of _____

(A) Tally

(B) Corel Draw

(C) Photoshop

(D) None of these

44.The _____ is a customizable toolbar that contains commands that you may want to use.

(A) View option toolbar

(B) Quick access toolbar

(C) Title bar

(D) Ribbon

45.Go to beginning of a document. press

(A) Home

(B) End

(C) Num Lock

(D) Tab

46.A(n) _____ lists the terms and topics that are discussed in a document, along with the pages that they appear on.

(A) Table

(B) Index

(C) Indent

(D) Contents

47.Microsoft Office is

(A) Shareware

(B) Public domain software

(C) An application suit

(D) Firmware

48.What is the default page size for word document?

(A) Letter

(B) A4

(C) Legal

(D) None of these

49.Where all the tabs (Ex. Home tab, insert tab, etc.) are located?

(A) Scroll bar

(B) Ribbon

(C) Title bar

(D) Status bar

50.____ refer to numbers that are positioned slightly higher or slightly lower than the text on the line respectively.

(A) Subscript and Superscript

(B) Superscript and Subscript

(C) Superiorscript and Subscript

(D) Subscript and Superiorscript

51.View the document as it would look as a webpage is

(A) Outline

(B) Print layout

(C) Full screen reading

(D) Web layout

52.One of the statement is incorrect?

(A) MS Word cannot add highlights.

(B) MS Word can check the spelling.

(C) Mailing tab is in MS Word 2007.

(D) In MS word we insert pictures.

53.The ______ feature in Word automatically corrects certain spelling, typing, and capitalisation or grammar errors.

(A) AutoCorrect

(B) AutoMark

(C) AutoSpell

(D) AutoFix

55.To make the selected text underline, the shortcut key is ______

(A) Ctrl + I

(B) Ctrl + Alt + K

(C) Ctrl + J

(D) Ctrl + U

56.Using Print Preview is useful. When you want to

(A) copy the document

(B) delete the document

(C) save the document

(D) view how the document will appear when printed

57.From which panel you can insert Header and Footer in MS Word 2007?

(A) Format panel

(B) Review panel

(C) Home Panel

(D) Insert panel

58.The shortcut key for copy selected text/picture in MS Word is

(A) Ctrl + C

(B) Ctrl + V

(C) Ctrl + X

(D) Ctrl + Y

59.In ______ we can see the status of the document.

(A) Menu bar

(B) Status bar

(C) Ribbon

(D) Title bar

60.What is a gallery of text styles that you can add to your documents to create decorative effects?

(A) Footer

(B) Header

(C) WordArt

(D) Clipart

61.What is gutter margin?

(A) Margin is added to the outside of the page when printing

(B) Margin that is added to the binding side of page when printing

(C) Margin that is added to right margin when printing

(D) Margin that is added to the left margin when printing

62.______ can use to navigate a long document through small pictures of each page.

(A) Thumbnails

(B) Document map

(C) Gridlines

(D) Ruler

63.A ______ is a visual representation of your information that you can quickly and easily create, choosing from among many different layouts, to effectively communicate your message or ideas.

(A) Hyperlink

(B) ClipArt

(C) SmartArt graphic

(D) Table

64.Press ______ to open 'Replace' dialog box.

(A) Alt + H

(B) Ctrl + H

(C) Ctrl + Alt + H

(D) Tab + H

65. Drop Cap is a formatting option in MS Word that allows you to insert a

(A) Fancy Small letter

(B) Normal Small letter

(C) Normal Capital letter

(D) All of these

66. Background color or effects applied on a document is not visible in

(A) Print Preview

(B) Reading view

(C) Web Layout view

(D) Print Layout view

67. What is place to the left of horizontal scroll bar?

(A) Indicators

(B) Insert tab

(C) View buttons

(D) Ribbon

68. What is the overall term for creating, editing, formatting, storing, retrieving and printing a text document?

(A) Database Management

(B) Web design

(C) Spreadsheet design

(D) Word processing

69.The shortcut key to open a new file in MS Word is

(A) Ctrl + N

(B) Ctrl + C

(C) Ctrl + V

(D) Ctrl + X

70.Press ______ to open 'Go' to dialog box.

(A) Ctrl + Alt + G

(B) Tab + G

(C) Ctrl + G

(D) Alt + G

71.Press ______ to open 'Find' dialog box.

(A) Ctrl + Alt + F

(B) Tab + F

(C) Alt + F

(D) Ctrl + F

72.To cut the selected text, these keys should be pressed

(A) Ctrl + C

(B) Ctrl + D

(C) Ctrl + V

(D) Ctrl + X

73.If you want to undo an action in a document, then press

(A) Ctrl + R

(B) Ctrl + U

(C) Ctrl + X

(D) Ctrl + Z

74.If you want to redo an action in a document, then press

(A) Ctrl + R

(B) Ctrl + U

(C) Ctrl + X

(D) Ctrl + Y

75.The shortcut key for paste selected text/picture in MS Word is

(A) Ctrl + C

(B) Ctrl + X

(C) Ctrl + Y

(D) Ctrl + Z

76.Just below the toolbar, there is a ______ bar.

(A) scroll

(B) task

(C) formula

(D) formatting bar

77.Turn on ______, which allows word to break lines between the syllables of words.

(A) Hyphenation

(B) Hyperlink

(C) Footer

(D) Header

78.Insert a ___ to illustrate and compare data.

(A) Hyperlink

(B) Footer

(C) Header

(D) Chart

79.____ refers to back the object to one level or to all objects.

(A) Align

(B) Rotate

(C) Bring to front

(D) Send to back

80.A memory bus is mainly used for communication between

(A) Processor and I/O devices

(B) Processor and memory

(C) Input devices and output devices

(D) I/O devices and SMPS

81.____ lines to drop for drop for drop cap.

(A) 2

(B) 3

(C) 4

(D) 5

82.____ refers to a title for a part of a document.

(A) Leader characters

(B) Indent

(C) Header

(D) Heading

83.In word, you can use styles to

(A) format documents

(B) delete text in documents

(C) save changes to documents

(D) makes copies of documents

84.Change the case of letters by

(A) Alt + F3

(B) Ctrl + F3

(C) Shift + F3

(D) Tab + F3

85.Which of the following are valid minimum and maximum zoom sizes in MS Word?

(A) 0, 100

(B) 0, 1000

(C) 10, 500

(D) 10, 100

86.What is the ghosted text or picture behind the content on the page?

(A) Clipart

(B) Watermark

(C) WordArt

(D) All of these

87.The key F12 opens a

(A) Close dialog box

(B) Save dialog box

(C) Open dialog box

(D) SavaAs dialog box

88.Which of the following option may be used to change page-size and margins?

(A) Data

(B) Tools

(C) View

(D) Page Setup

89.The software that is used to create text based document are referred to as

(A) DBMS

(B) Spreadsheet

(C) Word Processors

(D) Presentation

90.Which of the following is not a type of page margin?

(A) Top

(B) Center

(C) Left

(D) Right

91.In MS word we insert

(A) Page number

(B) Text Box

(C) Table

(D) All of these

92. What is used to measure and line up objects in the document?

(A) Ruler

(B) Gridlines

(C) Document map

(D) Thumbnails

93. Which is not a page size in MS Word document?

(A) A3

(B) A4

(C) Letter

(D) Z100

94. The process of making changes to an existing document is referred to as _____ it.

(A) creating

(B) editing

(C) changing

(D) modifying

95. User can use ______ commands to search for and correct words in a document.

(A) Copy and Paste

(B) Find and Replace

(C) Header and Footer

(D) Print and Print preview

96.For Paste, Special, the keyboard shortcut key is

(A) Tab + Alt + V

(B) Ctrl + Tab + V

(C) Ctrl + Delete + V

(D) Ctrl + Alt + V

97.Use ______ to follow hyperlink.

(A) Ctrl + Space

(B) Ctrl + Esc

(C) Ctrl + Click

(D) Ctrl + Enter

98.The processing of input to output is directed by _____

(A) Software

(B) Hardware

(C) Printer

(D) None of these

99.The CPU (central processing unit) consists of ______

(A) Input, output, and processing

(B) Control unit, primary storage, and secondary storage

(C) Control unit, arithmetic-logic unit, and primary storage

(D) None of these

100.The keyboard and mouse of a computer are the most commonly
used ___

(A) Input Unit

(B) Output unit

(C) Processing unit

(D) None of these

1.Which bar shows the current position as far the text goes?

(A) Title bar

(B) Menu bar

(C) Scroll bar

(D) Status bar

Ans: D

Status bar

2. Select all the text in MS Word document by

(A) Ctrl +S

(B) Ctrl+ 1

(C) Ctrl+ A

(D) Ctrl+ V

Ans: C

Ctrl+ A

3. _____ is not a part of a MS Word document

(A) Quick access toolbar

(B) Start Menu button

(C) Home panel

(D) View option

Ans: B

Start Menu button

4.The name of a word document displays in _____

(A) Ribbon

(B) Title bar

(C) Status bar

(D) Home tab

Ans: B

Title bar

5.Each line represents how many letters in WordStar?

(A) 20

(B) 35

(C) 65

(D) 75

Ans: C

65

6.What is the blank space outside the printing area on a page?

(A) Clipart

(B) Margins

(C) Header

(D) Footer

Ans: B

Margins

7.Which of the following is an example of page orientation?

(A) Landscape

(B) Subscript

(C) Superscript

(D) A4

Ans: A

Landscape

8.Formatting is performed on

(A) Text

(B) Table

(C) Menu

(D) Both (a) and (b)

Ans: D

Both (a) and (b)

9.Which of the following software is used for making resume?

(A) MS Excel

(B) MS Word

(C) Dev C

(D) Java

Ans: B

MS Word

10.Press _____ to open the help window in MS word document.

(A) F1

(B) F2

(C) F9

(D) F11

Ans: A

F1

11.Microsoft word is _____ software.

(A) Application

(B) Compiler

(C) System

(D) Programming

Ans: A

Application

12.Which is not in MS word?

(A) Italic

(B) Magic tool

(C) Font

(D) Bold

Ans: B

Magic tool

13.____ cannot be used to work in MS Office.

(A) Joystick

(B) Scanner

(C) Light Pen

(D) Mouse

Ans: A

Joystick

14.Which is not an edition of MS Word?

(A) MS Word 2003

(B) MS Word 2007

(C) MS Word 2010

(D) MS Word 1020

Ans: D

MS Word 1020

15.The ___ works with the standard Copy and Paste commands.

(A) View tab

(B) Paragraph dialog box

(C) Office Clipboard

(D) All of these

Ans: C

Office Clipboard

16.Line spacing is in the _____ of MS Word.

(A) Format tab

(B) View tab

(C) Insert tab

(D) Home tab

Ans: D

Home tab

17.____ button reduces the window to an icon but word still remains active.

(A) Close

(B) Restore

(C) Maximize

(D) Minimize

Ans: D

Minimize

18. Which term is not related with font?

(A) Font grammar

(B) Font color

(C) Font size

(D) Font face

Ans: A

Font grammar

19.____ Button brings word window to the maximum original size.

(A) Scroll

(B) Close

(C) Restore

(D) Minimize

Ans: C

Restore

20.What is the smallest width of a column?

(A) 0"

(B) 1"

(C) 0.5"

(D) 1.5"

Ans: C

0.5"

21.Arial, Cambria, Verdana, Times New Roman are the name of _____

(A) Highlights

(B) Font face

(C) Text

(D) Alignment

Ans: B

Font face

22.What feature adjusts the top and bottom margins so that the text is centred vertically on the printed page?

(A) Vertical centering

(B) Vertical justifying

(C) Vertical adjusting

(D) Dual centering

Ans: B

Vertical justifying

23. The feature that keeps track of the right margin is

(A) Left justified

(B) Ragged right

(C) Right justified

(D) Find and replace

Ans: B

Ragged right

24. To make the selected text bold, the shortcut key is _____

(A) Alt+ B

(B) Shift+ B

(C) Ctrl+ B

(D) Space +H

Ans: C

Ctrl+ B

25. Which file format cannot be added to a Word document?

(A) .png

(B) .jpg

(C) .kpz

(D) .gif

Ans: C

.kpz

26.The process of removing unwanted part of an image is called

A.Hiding

B.Bordering

C.Cropping

D.Cutting

Answer : Cropping

Ans : C

27.A detailed written description of the programming cycle and the program, along with the test results and a printout of the program is called ______

(A) Spreadsheets

(B) Reporting

(C) Output

(D) Documentation

Ans: D

Documentation

28.A word processor would be used best to

(A) paint a picture

(B) workout income and expenses

(C) draw a diagram

(D) type a story

Ans: D

type a story

29.______ are advanced features that can speed up editing or formatting you may perform often in a word document.

(A) Comment

(B) Track changes

(C) Ribbon

(D) Macros

Ans: D

Macros

30.To move data from one part of the document to another, following is used.

(A) Cut and Delete

(B) Cut and Paste

(C) Copy and Paste

(D) Copy and Undo

Ans: B

Cut and Paste

31.Go to end of a document, press ______

(A) Num Lock

(B) Tab

(C) End

(D) Home

Ans: C

End

32. Which of the following options is used to display information such a title, page number of the document?

(A) Auto Correct

(B) Header and Footer

(C) Thesaurus

(D) Insert Table

Ans: B

Header and Footer

33. What is a set of unified design elements that provides a look for your document by using color, fonts and graphics?

(A) Highlight

(B) Format painter

(C) Line spacing

(D) Theme

Ans: D

Theme

34. To align right the selected text, the shortcut key is

(A) Ctrl + L

(B) Ctrl + R

(C) Ctrl + J

(D) Ctrl + U

Ans: B

Ctrl + R

35. To align left the selected text, the shortcut key is

(A) Ctrl + L

(B) Ctrl + R

(C) Ctrl + J

(D) Ctrl + U

Ans: A

Ctrl + L

36.To specify margins in word, the user has to select Page Setup option from which menu?

(A) Auto correct

(B) Edit

(C) File

(D) Table

Ans: C

File

37.What is a note or annotation that an author or review adds to a document?

(A) Comment

(B) Caption

(C) Header

(D) Footer

Ans: A

Comment

38.Microsoft Office Word creates a _____ for you when you press ENTER or the SPACEBAR after you type the address of an existing Web page.

(A) Hyperlink

(B) Header

(C) Chart

(D) Footer

Ans: A

Hyperlink

39.Zoom in and out button is available on

(A) Scroll bar

(B) Home tab

(C) Page lauout tab

(D) View option toolbar

Ans: D

View option toolbar

40.What is the blinking symbol on the screen that shows where the next character will appear?

(A) Cursor

(B) Delete key

(C) Arrow key

(D) Return key

Ans: A

Cursor

41.The document can be zoom maximum upto

(A) 150%

(B) 200%

(C) 400%

(D) 500%

Ans: D

500%

42.The bar at the top of the window that bears the name of the window is known as

(A) Title bar

(B) Menu bar

(C) Status bar

(D) Control panel

Ans: A

Title bar

43.SmartArt is the feature of ____

(A) Tally

(B) Corel Draw

(C) Photoshop

(D) None of these

Ans: D

None of these

44.The ____ is a customizable toolbar that contains commands that you may want to use.

(A) View option toolbar

(B) Quick access toolbar

(C) Title bar

(D) Ribbon

Ans: B

Quick access toolbar

45.Go to beginning of a document. press

(A) Home

(B) End

(C) Num Lock

(D) Tab

Ans: A

Home

46.A(n) _____ lists the terms and topics that are discussed in a document, along with the pages that they appear on.

(A) Table

(B) Index

(C) Indent

(D) Contents

Ans: B

Index

47.Microsoft Office is

(A) Shareware

(B) Public domain software

(C) An application suit

(D) Firmware

Ans: C

An application suit

48.What is the default page size for word document?

(A) Letter

(B) A4

(C) Legal

(D) None of these

Ans: A

Letter

49.Where all the tabs (Ex. Home tab, insert tab, etc.) are located?

(A) Scroll bar

(B) Ribbon

(C) Title bar

(D) Status bar

Ans: B

Ribbon

50.____ refer to numbers that are positioned slightly higher or slightly lower than the text on the line respectively.

(A) Subscript and Superscript

(B) Superscript and Subscript

(C) Superiorscript and Subscript

(D) Subscript and Superiorscript

Ans: B

Superscript and Subscript

51.View the document as it would look as a webpage is

(A) Outline

(B) Print layout

(C) Full screen reading

(D) Web layout

Ans: D

Web layout

52.One of the statement is incorrect?

(A) MS Word cannot add highlights.

(B) MS Word can check the spelling.

(C) Mailing tab is in MS Word 2007.

(D) In MS word we insert pictures.

Ans: B

MS Word can check the spelling.

53.The _______ feature in Word automatically corrects certain spelling, typing, and capitalisation or grammar errors.

(A) AutoCorrect

(B) AutoMark

(C) AutoSpell

(D) AutoFix

Ans: A

AutoCorrect

55.To make the selected text underline, the shortcut key is ______

(A) Ctrl + I

(B) Ctrl + Alt + K

(C) Ctrl + J

(D) Ctrl + U

Ans: D

Ctrl + U

56.Using Print Preview is useful. When you want to

(A) copy the document

(B) delete the document

(C) save the document

(D) view how the document will appear when printed

Ans: D

view how the document will appear when printed

57.From which panel you can insert Header and Footer in MS Word 2007?

(A) Format panel

(B) Review panel

(C) Home Panel

(D) Insert panel

Ans: D

Insert panel

58.The shortcut key for copy selected text/picture in MS Word is

(A) Ctrl + C

(B) Ctrl + V

(C) Ctrl + X

(D) Ctrl + Y

Ans: A

Ctrl + C

59.In _____ we can see the status of the document.

(A) Menu bar

(B) Status bar

(C) Ribbon

(D) Title bar

Ans: B

Status bar

60.What is a gallery of text styles that you can add to your documents to create decorative effects?

(A) Footer

(B) Header

(C) WordArt

(D) Clipart

Ans: C

WordArt

61.What is gutter margin?

(A) Margin is added to the outside of the page when printing

(B) Margin that is added to the binding side of page when printing

(C) Margin that is added to right margin when printing

(D) Margin that is added to the left margin when printing

Ans: D

Margin that is added to the left margin when printing

62.______ can use to navigate a long document through small pictures of each page.

(A) Thumbnails

(B) Document map

(C) Gridlines

(D) Ruler

Ans: A

Thumbnails

63.A ______ is a visual representation of your information that you can quickly and easily create, choosing from among many different layouts, to effectively communicate your message or ideas.

(A) Hyperlink

(B) ClipArt

(C) SmartArt graphic

(D) Table

Ans: B

ClipArt

64.Press _______ to open 'Replace' dialog box.

(A) Alt + H

(B) Ctrl + H

(C) Ctrl + Alt + H

(D) Tab + H

Ans: B

Ctrl + H

65.Drop Cap is a formatting option in MS Word that allows you to insert a

(A) Fancy Small letter

(B) Normal Small letter

(C) Normal Capital letter

(D) All of these

Ans: D

All of these

66.Background color or effects applied on a document is not visible in

(A) Print Preview

(B) Reading view

(C) Web Layout view

(D) Print Layout view

Ans: A

Print Preview

67.What is place to the left of horizontal scroll bar?

(A) Indicators

(B) Insert tab

(C) View buttons

(D) Ribbon

Ans: C

View buttons

68.What is the overall term for creating, editing, formatting, storing, retrieving and printing a text document?

(A) Database Management

(B) Web design

(C) Spreadsheet design

(D) Word processing

Ans: D

Word processing

69.The shortcut key to open a new file in MS Word is

(A) Ctrl + N

(B) Ctrl + C

(C) Ctrl + V

(D) Ctrl + X

Ans: A

Ctrl + N

70.Press ______ to open 'Go' to dialog box.

(A) Ctrl + Alt + G

(B) Tab + G

(C) Ctrl + G

(D) Alt + G

Ans: C

Ctrl + G

71.Press _____ to open 'Find' dialog box.

(A) Ctrl + Alt + F

(B) Tab + F

(C) Alt + F

(D) Ctrl + F

Ans: D

Ctrl + F

72.To cut the selected text, these keys should be pressed

(A) Ctrl + C

(B) Ctrl + D

(C) Ctrl + V

(D) Ctrl + X

Ans: D

Ctrl + X

73.If you want to undo an action in a document, then press

(A) Ctrl + R

(B) Ctrl + U

(C) Ctrl + X

(D) Ctrl + Z

Ans: D

Ctrl + Z

74. If you want to redo an action in a document, then press

(A) Ctrl + R

(B) Ctrl + U

(C) Ctrl + X

(D) Ctrl + Y

Ans: D

Ctrl + Y

75. The shortcut key for paste selected text/picture in MS Word is

(A) Ctrl + C

(B) Ctrl + X

(C) Ctrl + Y

(D) Ctrl + Z

Ans: B

Ctrl + X

76. Just below the toolbar, there is a _______ bar.

(A) scroll

(B) task

(C) formula

(D) formatting bar

Ans: D

formatting bar

77.Turn on ______, which allows word to break lines between the syllables of words.

(A) Hyphenation

(B) Hyperlink

(C) Footer

(D) Header

Ans: A

Hyphenation

78.Insert a ___ to illustrate and compare data.

(A) Hyperlink

(B) Footer

(C) Header

(D) Chart

Ans: D

Chart

79.____ refers to back the object to one level or to all objects.

(A) Align

(B) Rotate

(C) Bring to front

(D) Send to back

Ans: D

Send to back

80.A memory bus is mainly used for communication between

(A) Processor and I/O devices

(B) Processor and memory

(C) Input devices and output devices

(D) I/O devices and SMPS

Ans: B

Processor and memory

81.____ lines to drop for drop for drop cap.

(A) 2

(B) 3

(C) 4

(D) 5

Ans: B

3

82.____ refers to a title for a part of a document.

(A) Leader characters

(B) Indent

(C) Header

(D) Heading

Ans: D

Heading

83.In word, you can use styles to

(A) format documents

(B) delete text in documents

(C) save changes to documents

(D) makes copies of documents

Ans: A

format documents

84.Change the case of letters by

(A) Alt + F3

(B) Ctrl + F3

(C) Shift + F3

(D) Tab + F3

Ans: C

Shift + F3

85.Which of the following are valid minimum and maximum zoom sizes in MS Word?

(A) 0, 100

(B) 0, 1000

(C) 10, 500

(D) 10, 100

Ans: C

10, 500

86.What is the ghosted text or picture behind the content on the page?

(A) Clipart

(B) Watermark

(C) WordArt

(D) All of these

Ans: B

Watermark

87.The key F12 opens a

(A) Close dialog box

(B) Save dialog box

(C) Open dialog box

(D) SavaAs dialog box

Ans: B

SavaAs dialog box

88.Which of the following option may be used to change page-size and margins?

(A) Data

(B) Tools

(C) View

(D) Page Setup

Ans: D

Page Setup

89.The software that is used to create text based document are referred to as

(A) DBMS

(B) Spreadsheet

(C) Word Processors

(D) Presentation

Ans: C

Word Processors

90.Which of the following is not a type of page margin?

(A) Top

(B) Center

(C) Left

(D) Right

Ans: C

Left

91.In MS word we insert

(A) Page number

(B) Text Box

(C) Table

(D) All of these

Ans: D

All of these

92.What is used to measure and line up objects in the document?

(A) Ruler

(B) Gridlines

(C) Document map

(D) Thumbnails

Ans: A

Ruler

93.Which is not a page size in MS Word document?

(A) A3

(B) A4

(C) Letter

(D) Z100

Ans: D

Z100

94.The process of making changes to an existing document is referred to as _____ it.

(A) creating

(B) editing

(C) changing

(D) modifying

Ans: B

editing

95.User can use ______ commands to search for and correct words in a document.

(A) Copy and Paste

(B) Find and Replace

(C) Header and Footer

(D) Print and Print preview

Ans: B

Find and Replace

96.For Paste, Special, the keyboard shortcut key is

(A) Tab + Alt + V

(B) Ctrl + Tab + V

(C) Ctrl + Delete + V

(D) Ctrl + Alt + V

Ans: D

Ctrl + Alt + V

97.Use _____ to follow hyperlink.

(A) Ctrl + Space

(B) Ctrl + Esc

(C) Ctrl + Click

(D) Ctrl + Enter

Ans: C

Ctrl + Click

98.The processing of input to output is directed by _____

(A) Software

(B) Hardware

(C) Printer

(D) None of these

Ans: A

Software

99.The CPU (central processing unit) consists of ______

(A) Input, output, and processing

(B) Control unit, primary storage, and secondary storage

(C) Control unit, arithmetic-logic unit, and primary storage

(D) None of these

Ans: C

Control unit, arithmetic-logic unit, and primary storage

100.The keyboard and mouse of a computer are the most commonly used ___

(A) Input Unit

(B) Output unit

(C) Processing unit

(D) None of these

Ans: D

None of these

www.ingramcontent.com/pod-product-compliance
Lightning Source LLC
Chambersburg PA
CBHW082115170726
47999CB00015BA/3076